HOW TO DRAW SUPERCHARACTERS™ AND SUPERMONSTERS™

EARL R. PHELPS

HOW TO DRAW SUPERCHARACTERS™ AND SUPERMONSTERS™

by Earl R. Phelps

Published by
Phelps Publishing
P.O. Box 22401
Cleveland, Ohio 44122

Library of Congress Catalog Card Number: 98-91317

ISBN 1-887627-03-0

Printed in the United States of America.

TABLE OF CONTENTS

Introduction

Hello Artist. Get ready to go on an exciting adventure into the art of drawing. This book will teach you how to draw and create your own Supercharcters and Supermonsters, Buildings and Streets, including a section on Drawing Your Own Comic Book.

It was my first time attending school that I can remember picking up a pencil and drawing. My Kindergarten Teacher drew a picture of an elephant and had everyone in the classroom draw it, I've been drawing ever since.

At the age of nine I became interest in comic books, I was never a comic book collector, say this because I would buy a book primarily on the merit of the artwork rather than the characters(s) or storyline of the book. I drew the characters of the books I bought, but after awhile I started creating my own Supercharacters, it was more fun.

I made this book for all of those who are intersted in learning how to draw and create their own Superchacacters and those who are already doing so. This book is comprised of three previous books I created, *How To Draw Your Own Supercharacters, How To Draw Your Own Supercharacters book II,* and *How To Draw Your Own Supermonsters.* If only I could have had a book like this when I was growing up, it would have made it much easier for me in learning how to draw.

This book has very few words because the illustrations speak for themselves. This was done to induce you to pick up a pencil and start drawing. The only way you can learn how to draw is to draw. To improve your artwork or anything in life, you must practice and study your craft. The purpose of this book is to implement practice, practice, and more practice in learning how to draw your own Supercharacters.

I've said enough! Let's get busy and have some fun!

Earl R. Phelps
Cleveland, Ohio

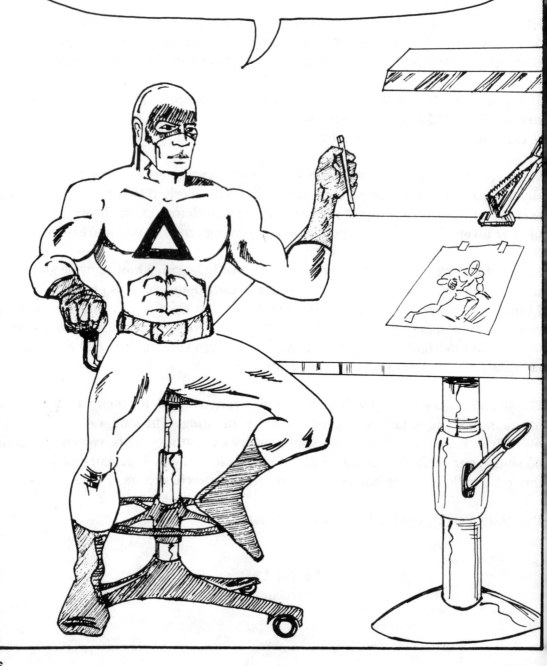

LOOSEN-UP EXERCISE

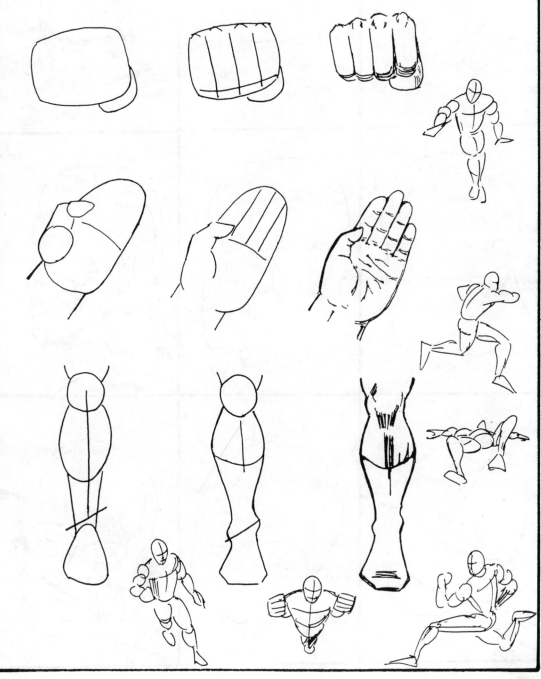

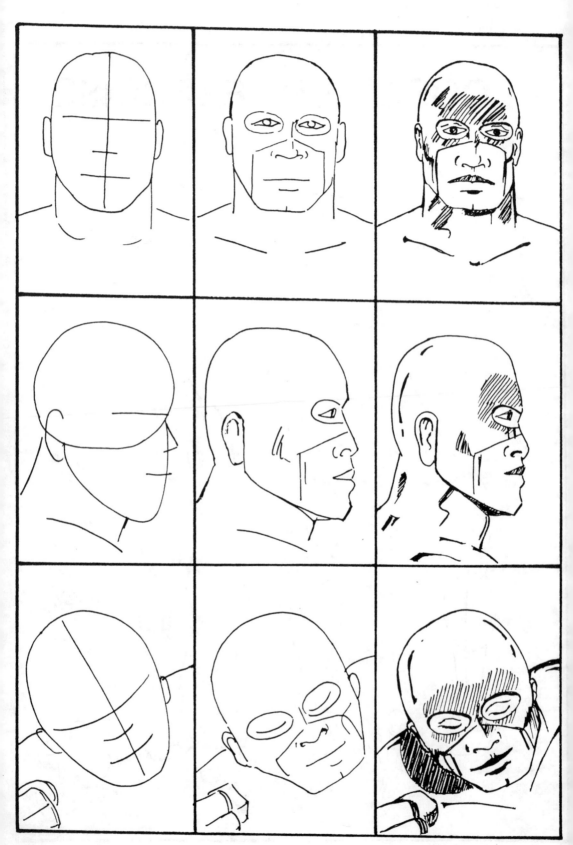

FACIAL EXPRESSIONS

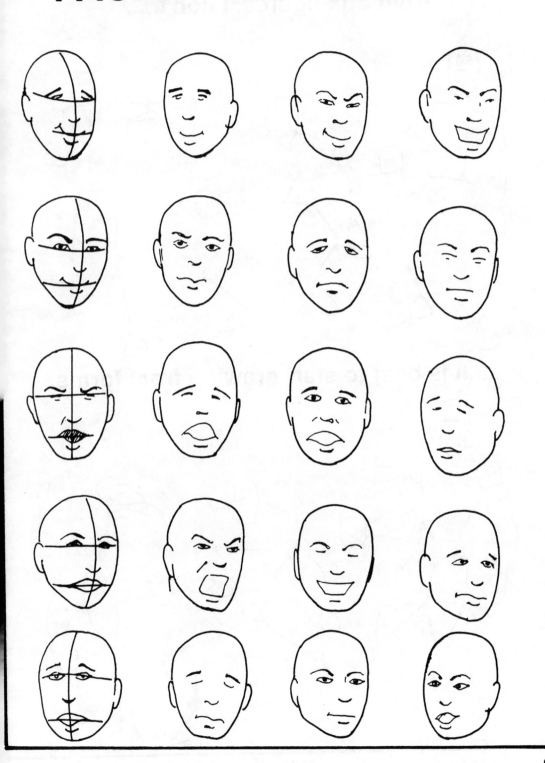

Some like to start drawing human forms from Stix figures. I don't.....

.....It is best to start drawing from forms.

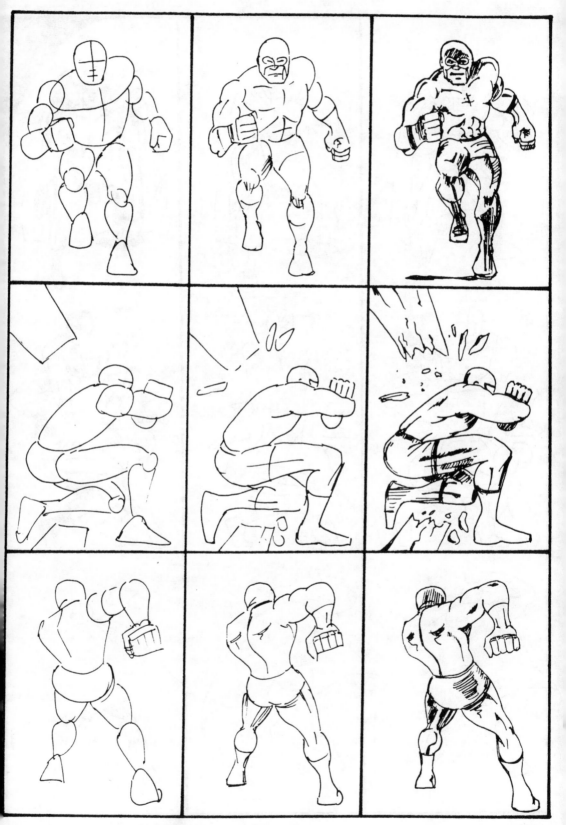

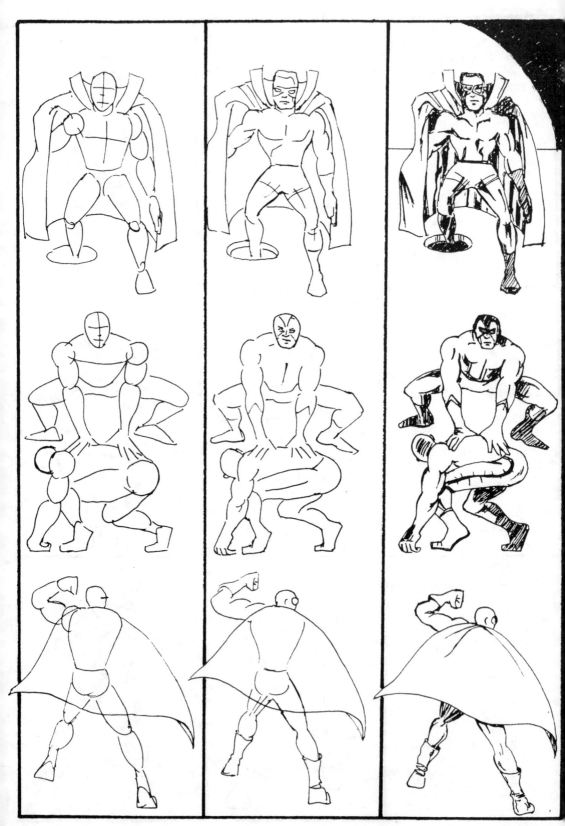

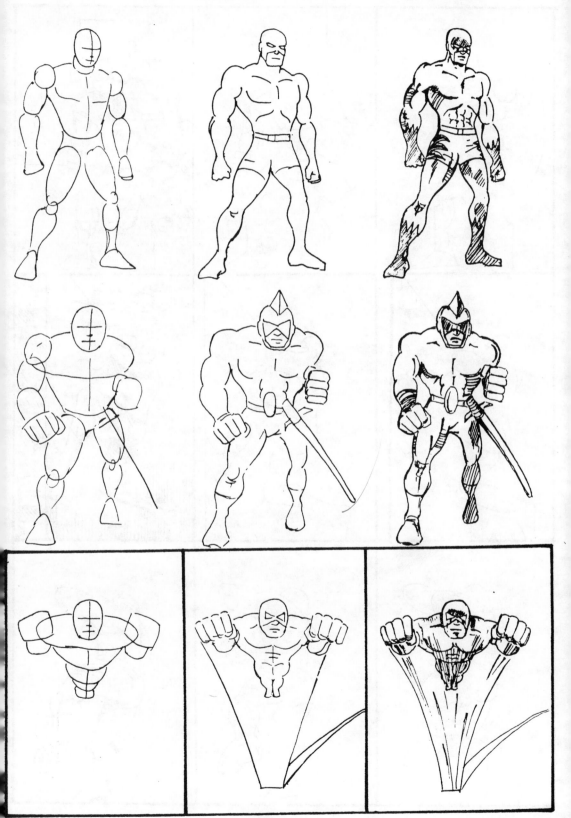

13

14

Let's Loosen-Up Again, just relax and start scribbling.

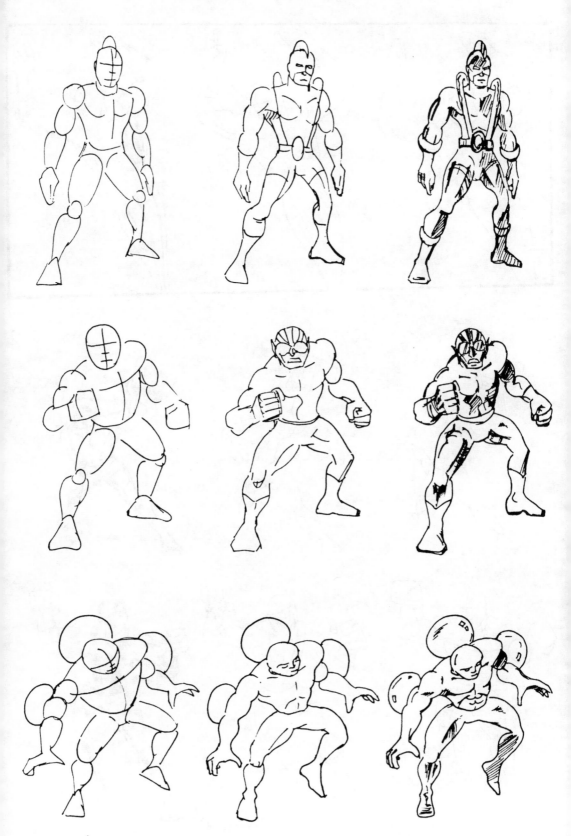

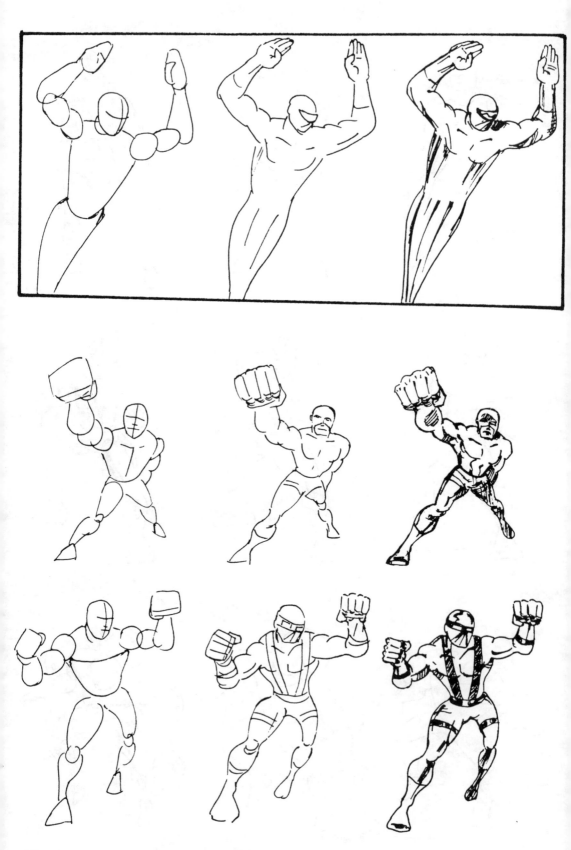

Construct the Drawings below in forms (as I have done throughout this book), and bring it to a complete finish as it is below.

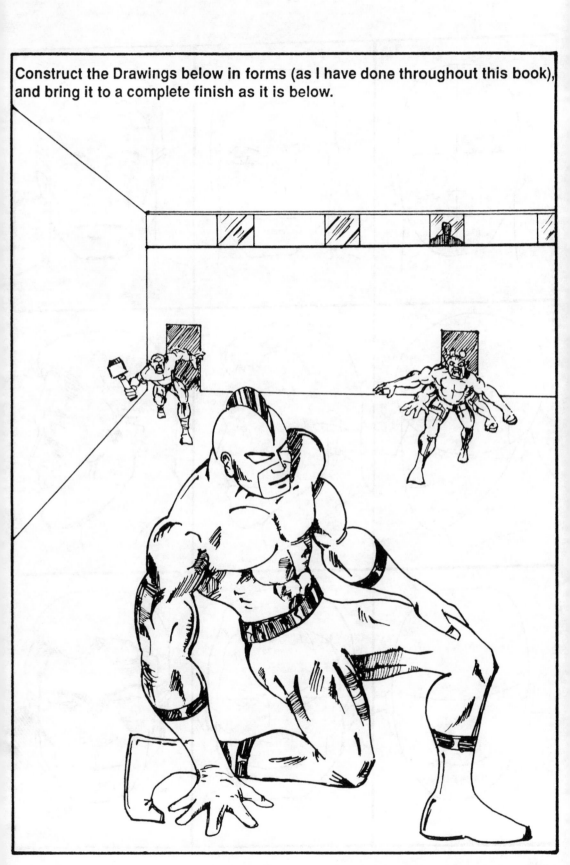

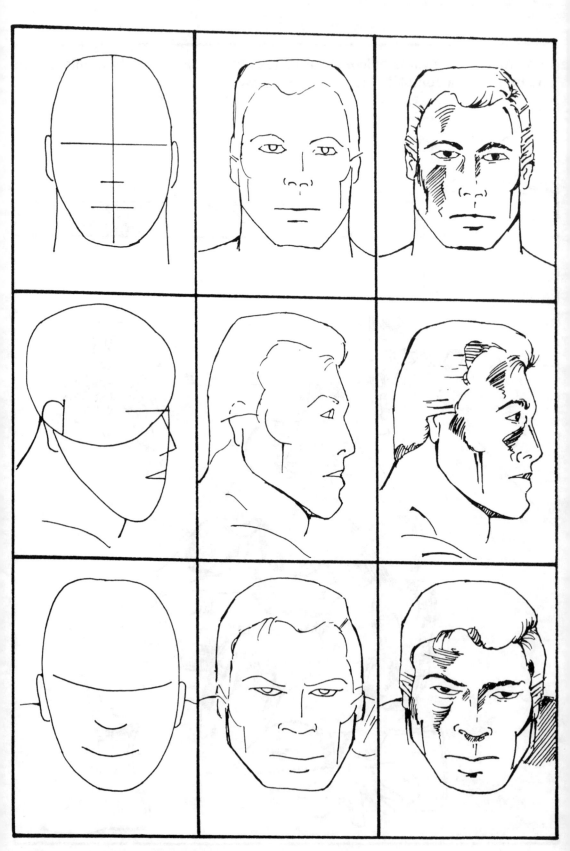

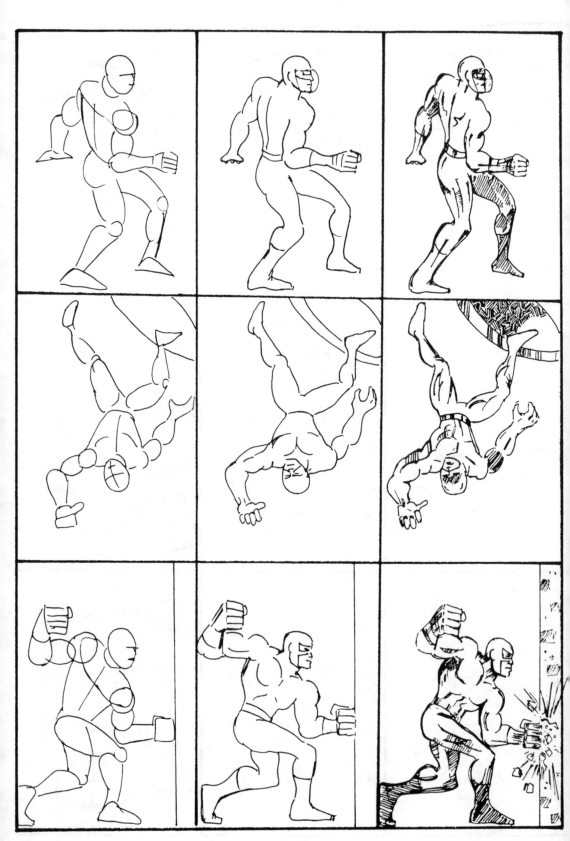

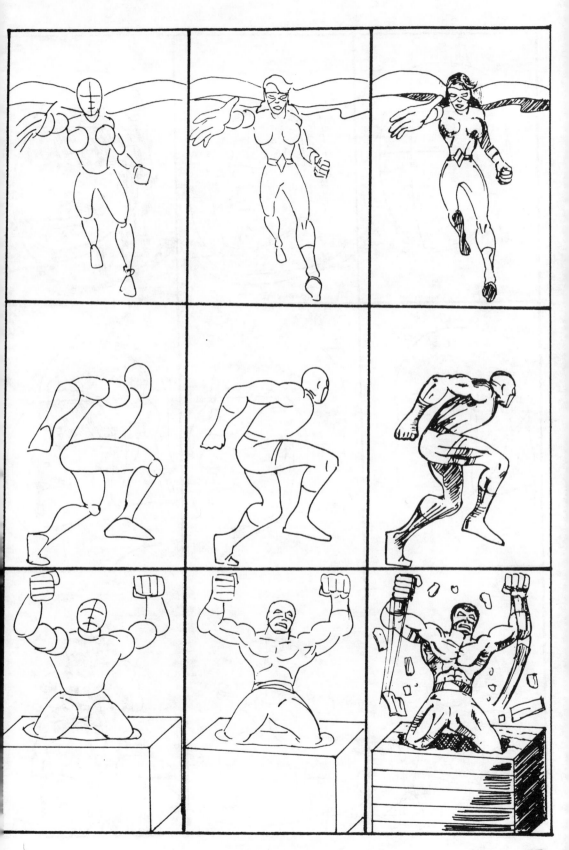

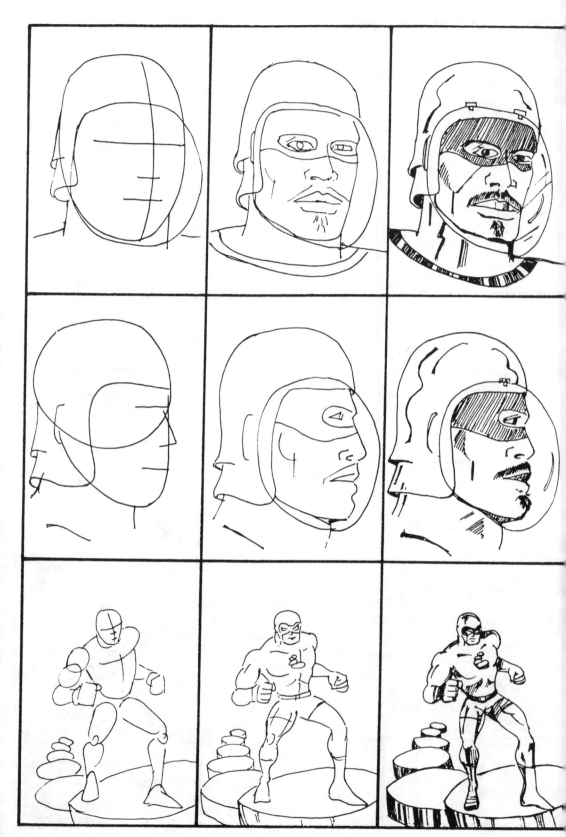

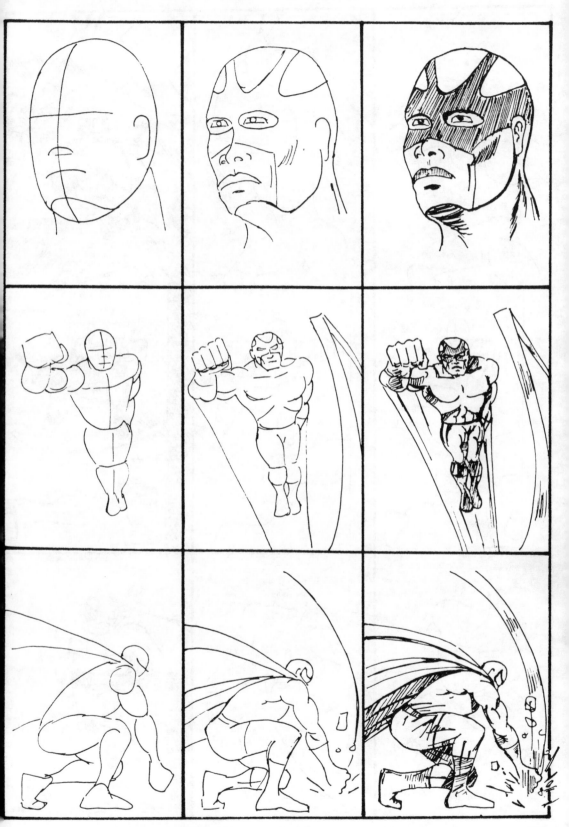

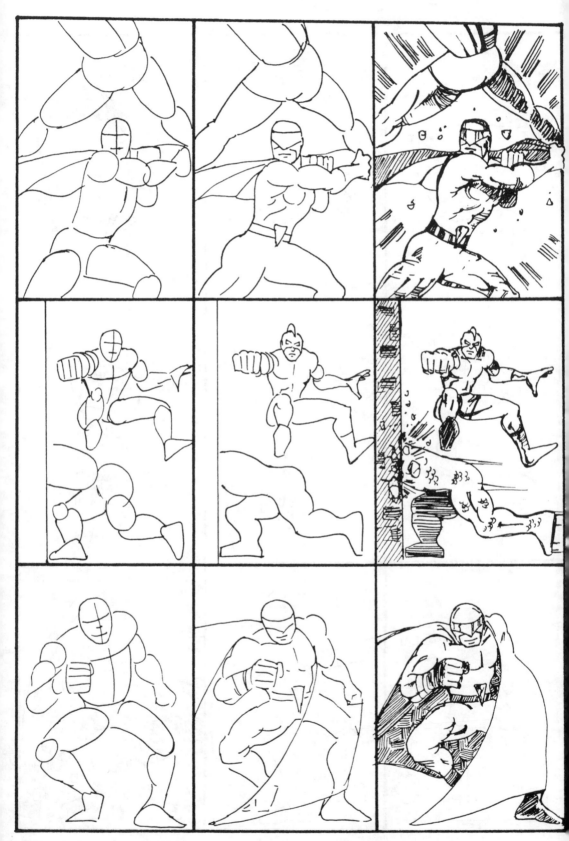

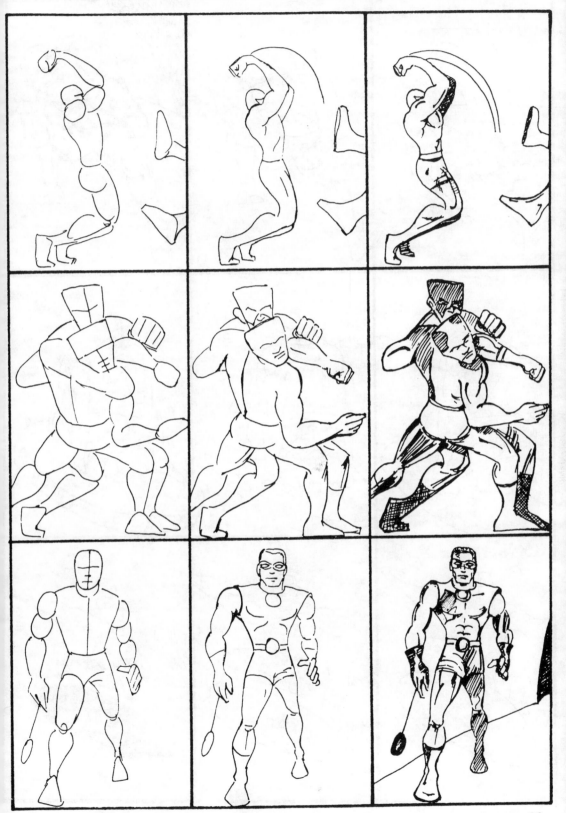

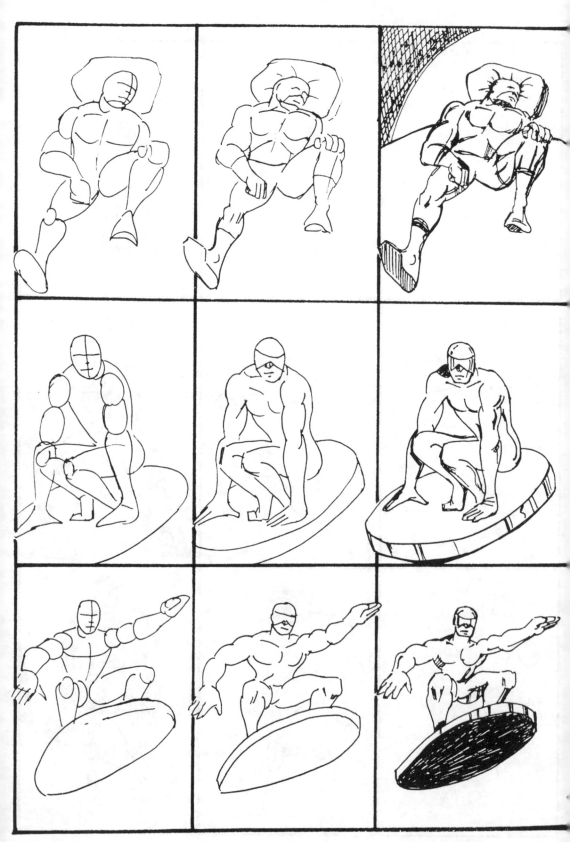

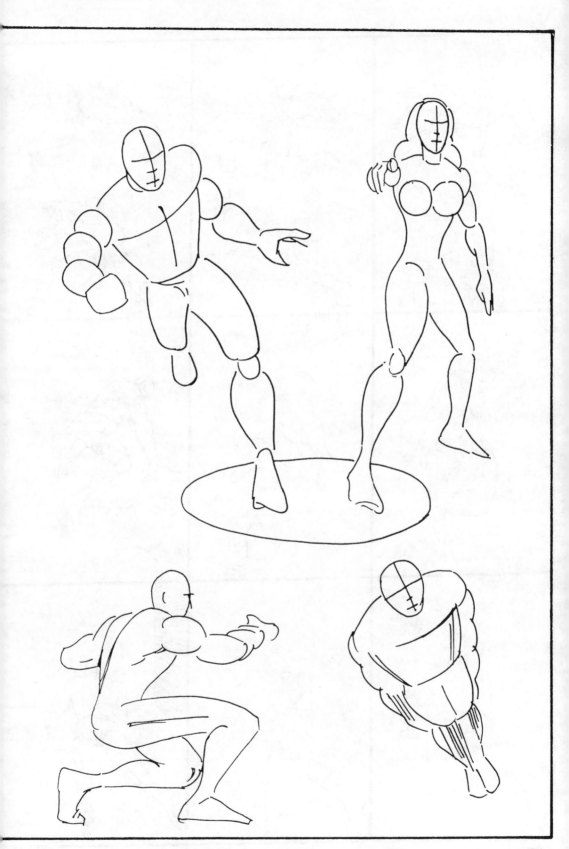

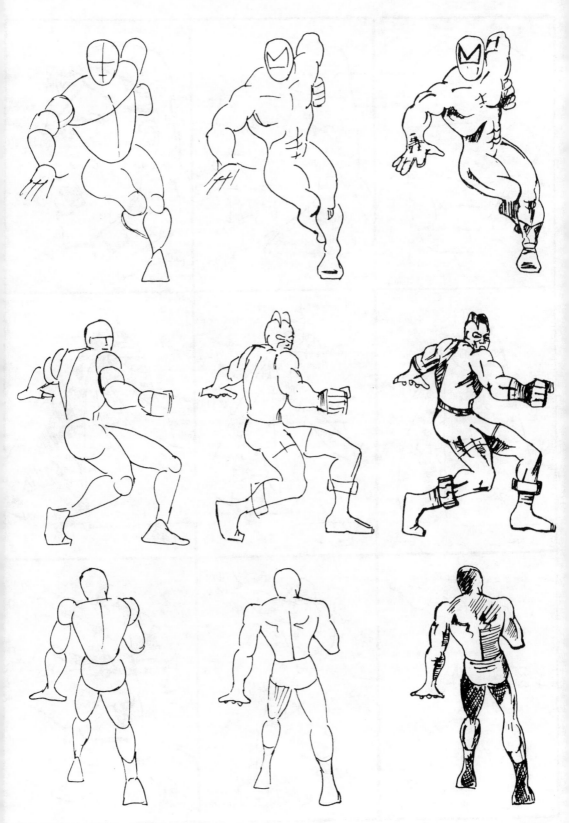

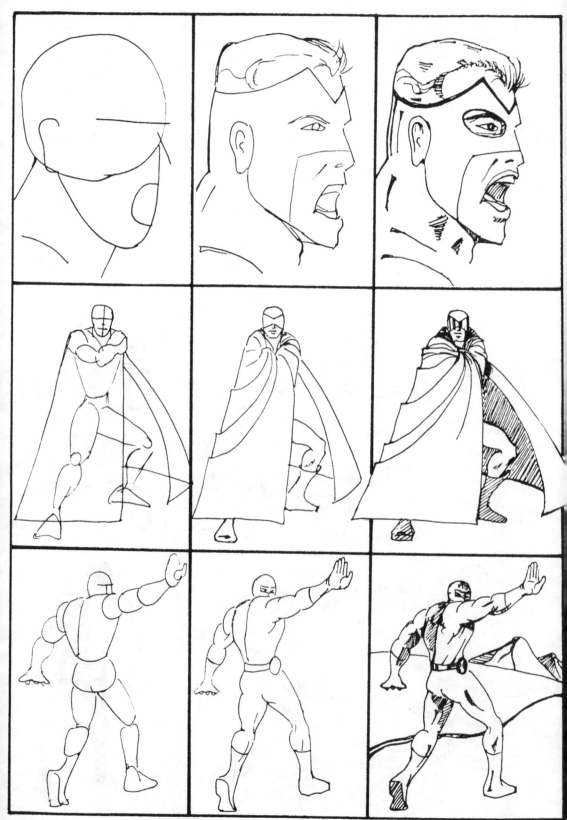

DRAWING THE HANDS

To improve on drawing the hand, practice on your own.

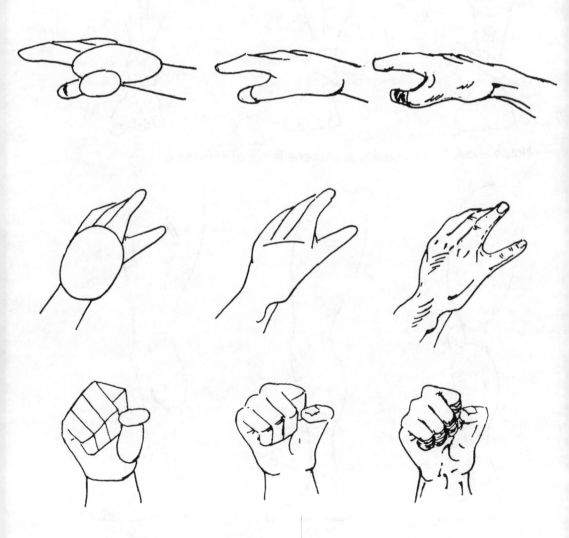

LEGS AND FEET

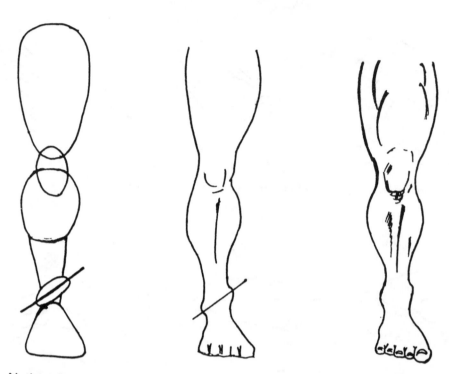

Notice above how the inside ankle bone is higher than the outside

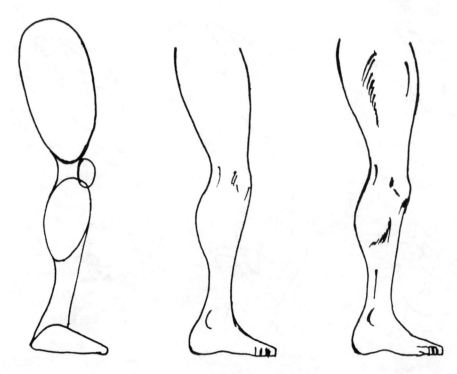

36

DRAWING THE ARMS

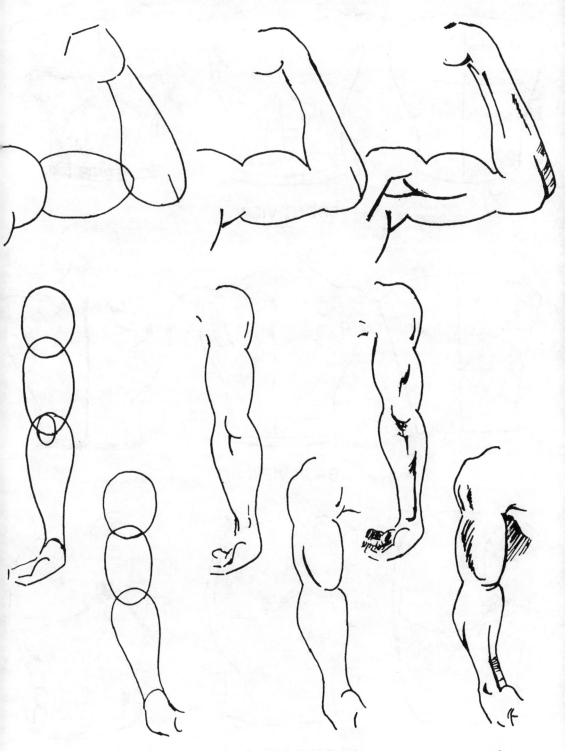

When drawing the arms, try to attain the essence of the curves and contours of the arms and muscles.

THE TORSO

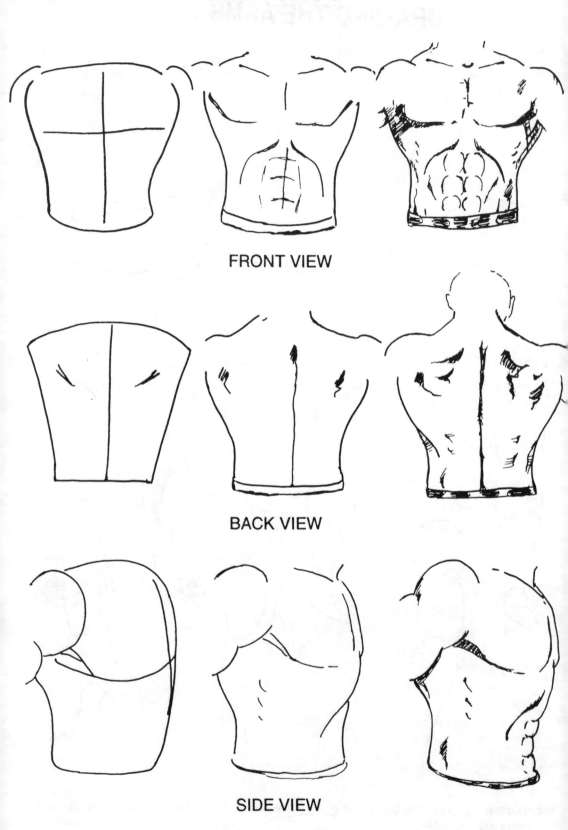

FRONT VIEW

BACK VIEW

SIDE VIEW

DRAWING THE HEAD AND FACE

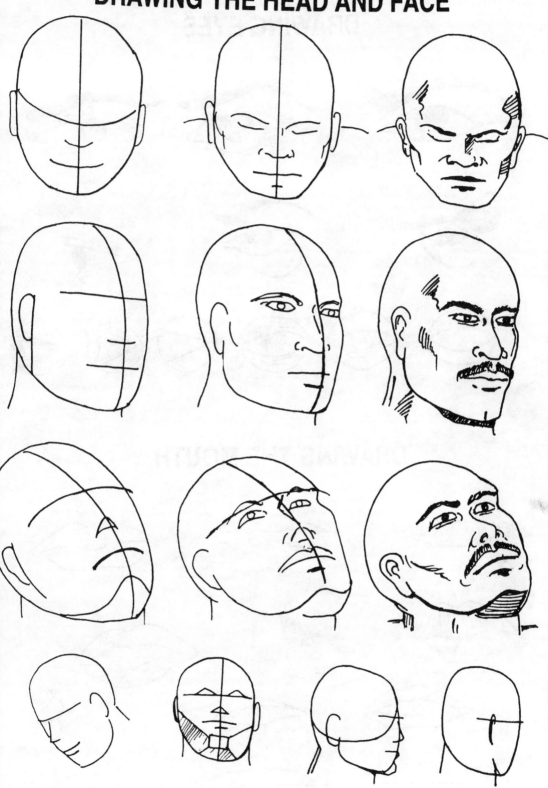

DRAWING EYES

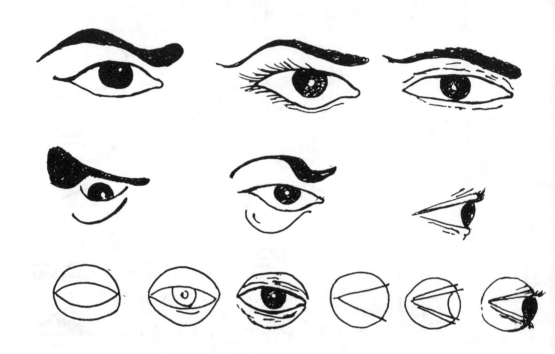

DRAWING THE MOUTH

THE MALE FIGURE

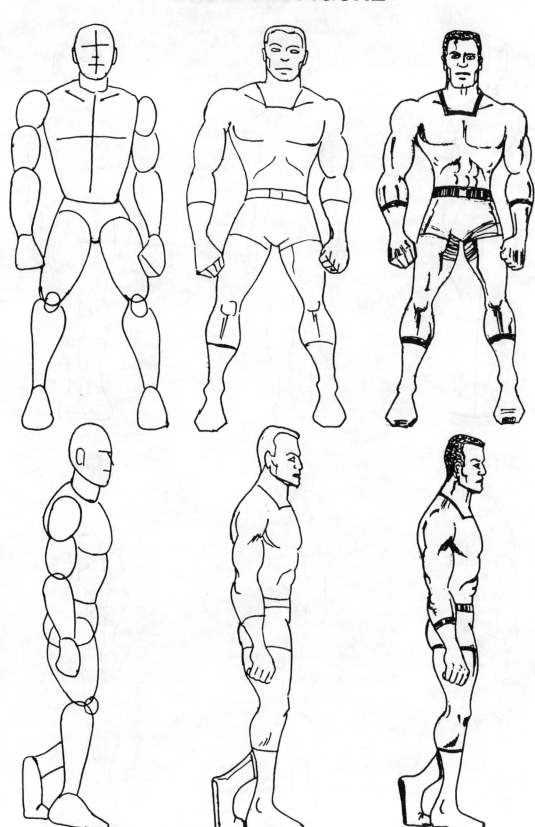

THE FEMALE FIGURE

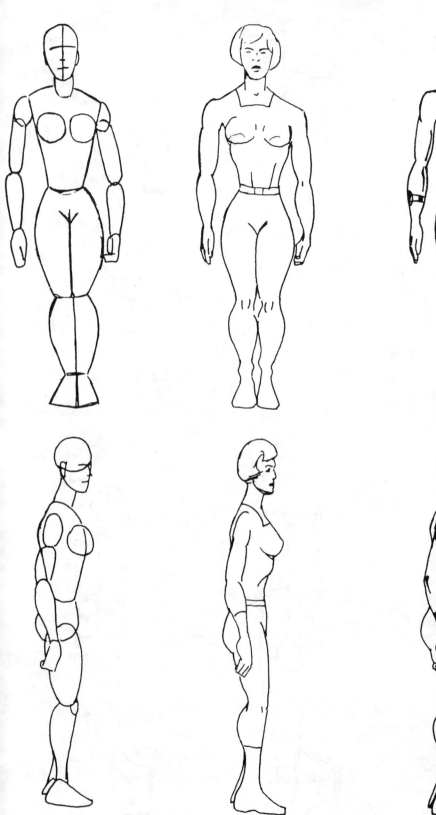

DRAWING SUPERMONSTERS

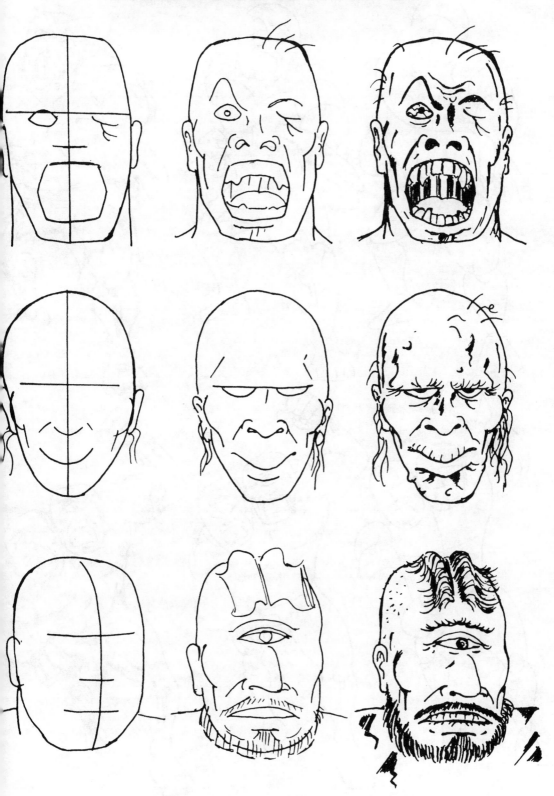

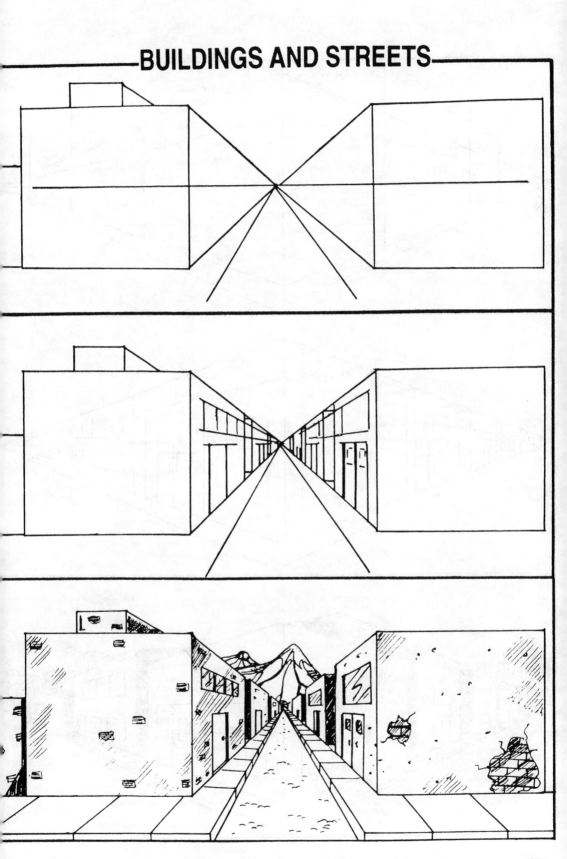

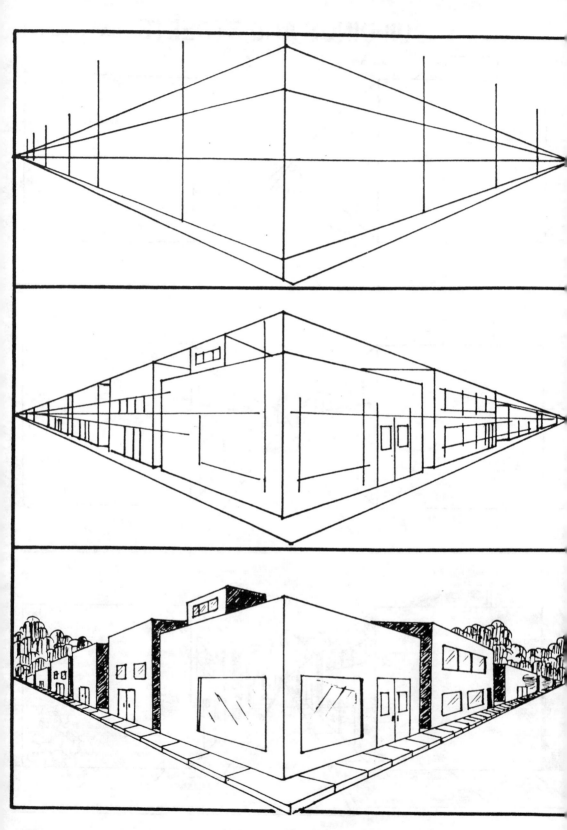

48

SUPERCHARACTER WOMEN

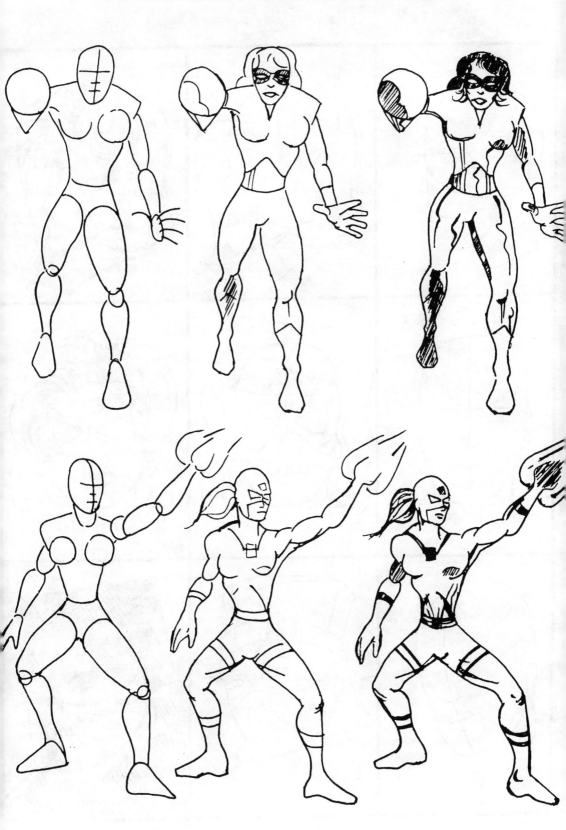

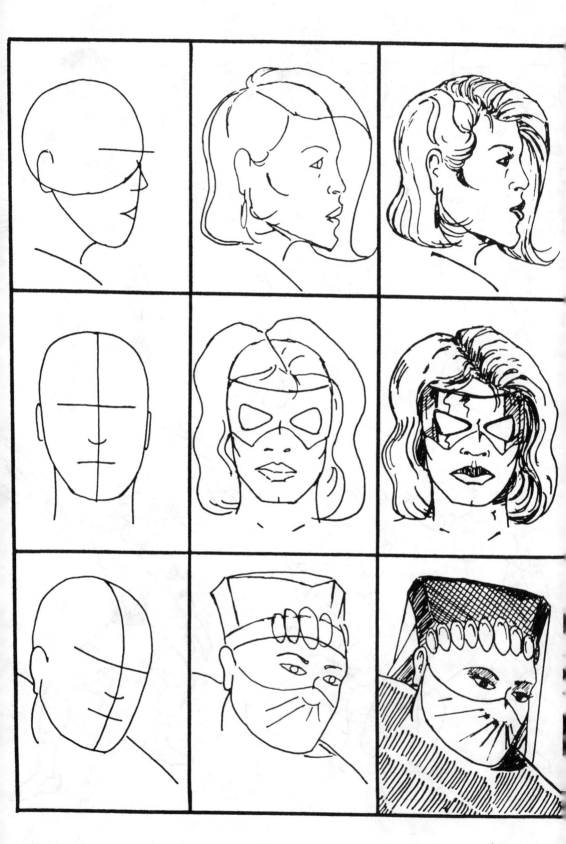

SUPERCHARACTERS
IN
ACTION!!

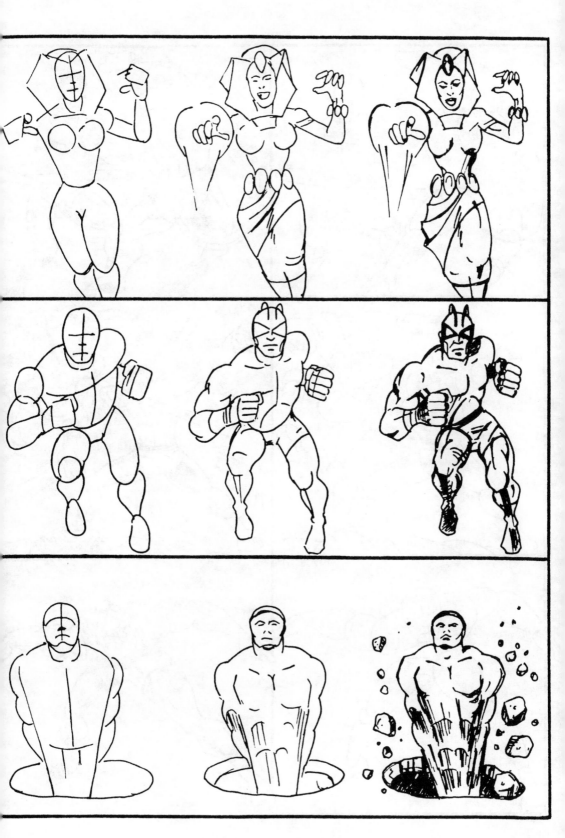

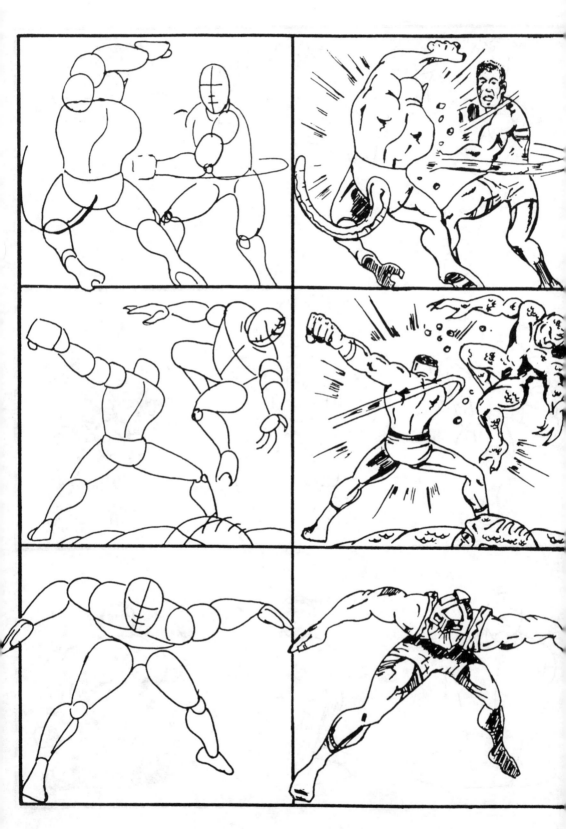

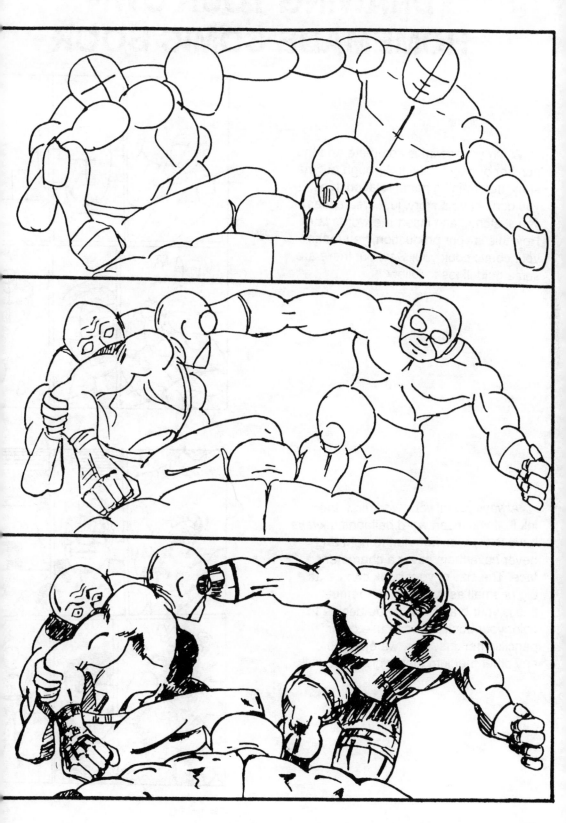

DRAWING YOUR OWN HOMEMADE COMIC BOOK

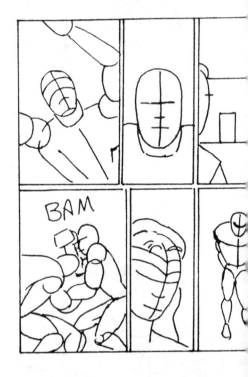

When your script is complete and the number of pages decided, rough out the story, determining panel relationships. If you don't have a story, just create it as you sketch it, and insert the words later. Hey, this is your production, you make your comic book your way, but there are some guidelines to follow.

Always pencil your work first, then ink it. If you insert word balloons, always have them read from left to right and never have them cover a character's face. The size of your book can be as big or small as you want, remember this is your brainchild. If you decide to color your book, you can use color pencils, markers, inks, watercolors or any other medium that might work well.

When drawing your cover, always leave enough space for the title of your book. Make your cover as exciting and interesting as possible without giving away the ending, or tip the reader off to any surprises in the story.

By practicing and studying the drawing techniques in this book, you will be able to create your own comic books, as well as draw the human figure better.

SO, LET'S KEEP BUSY !

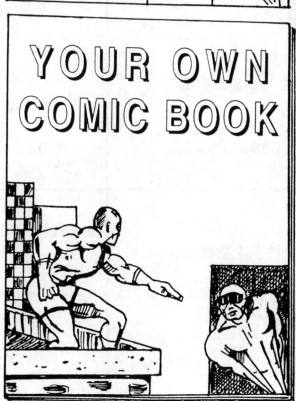

DRAWING MORE SUPERMONSTERS

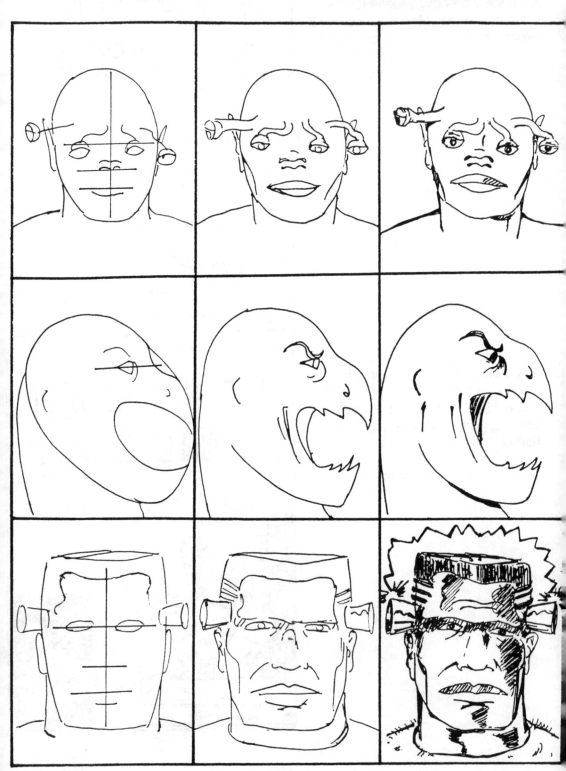

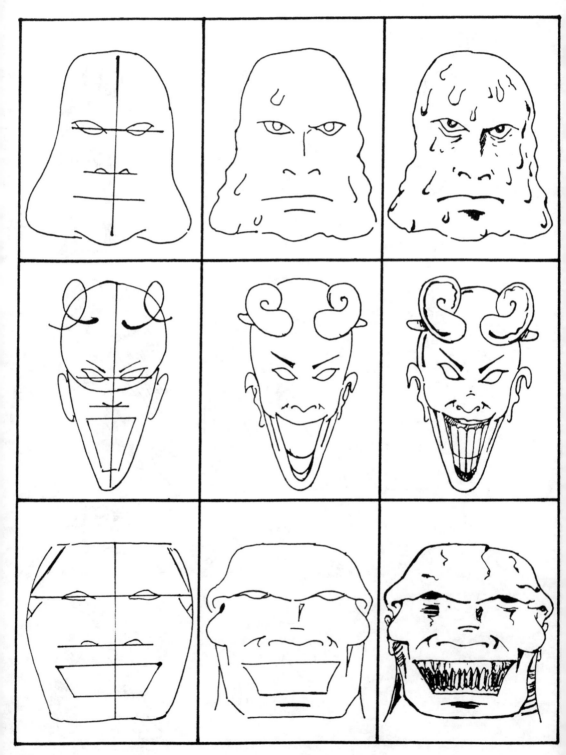

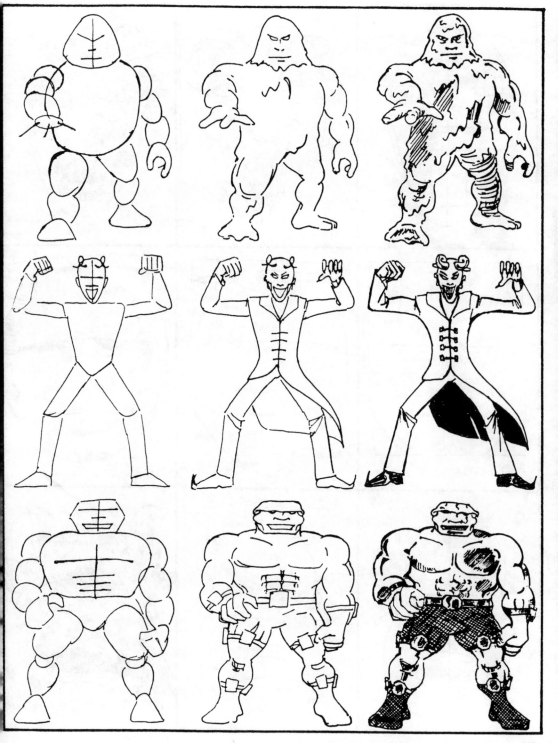

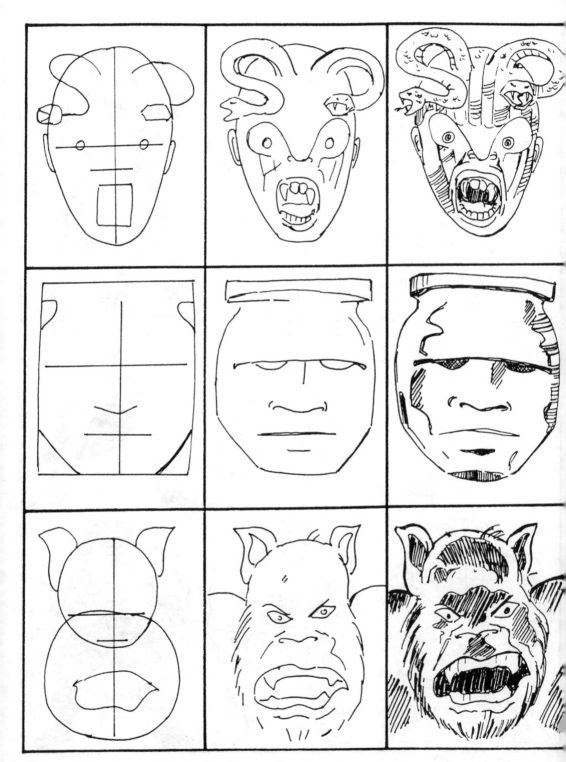

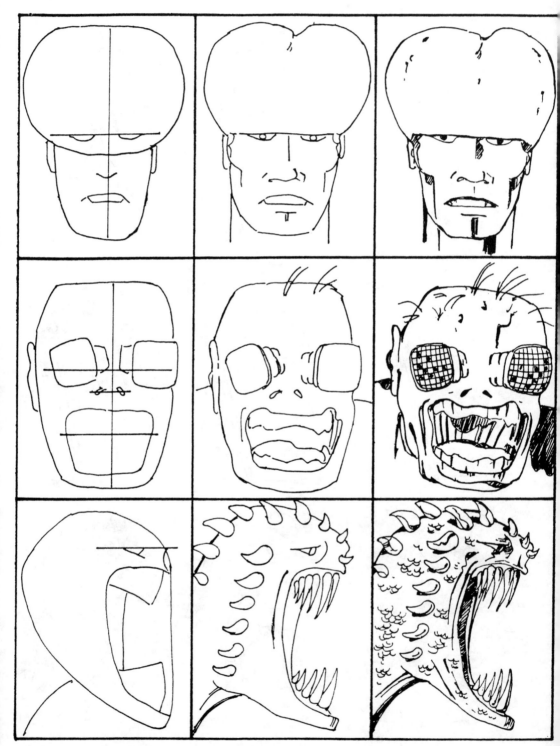

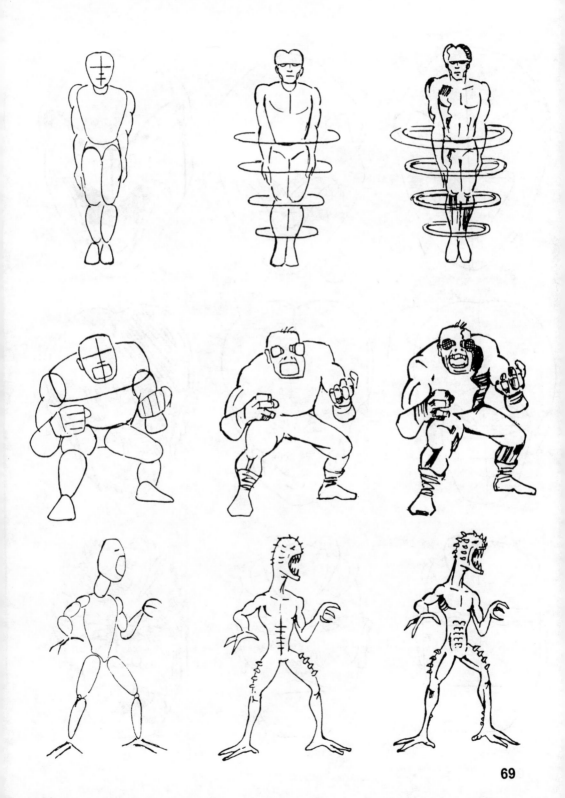

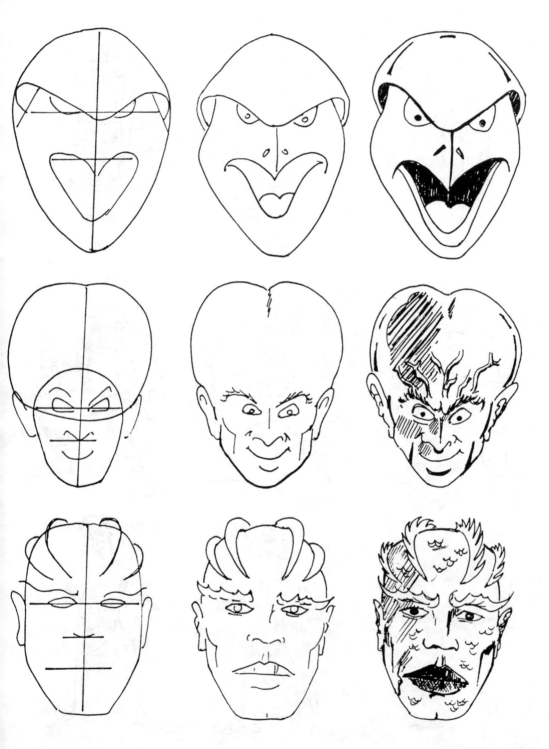

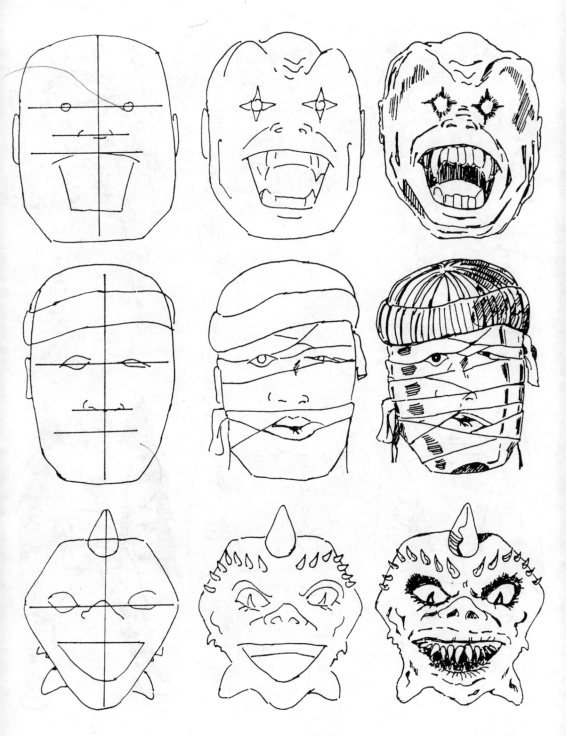

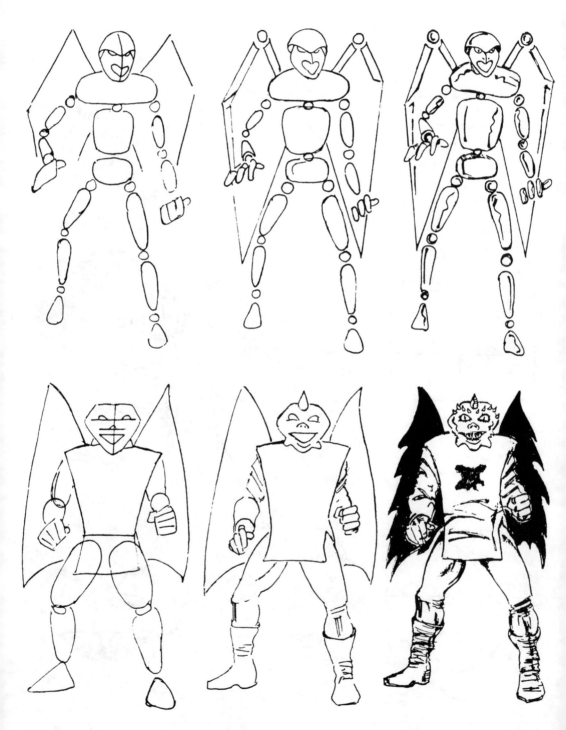

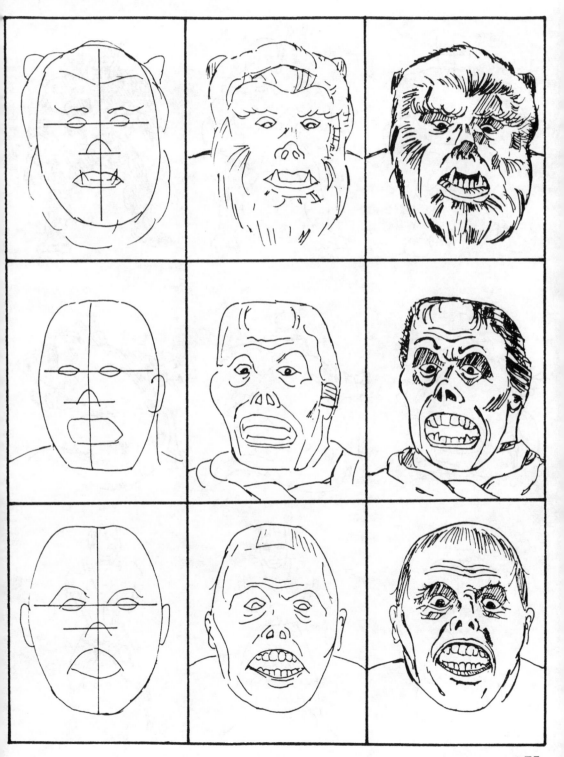

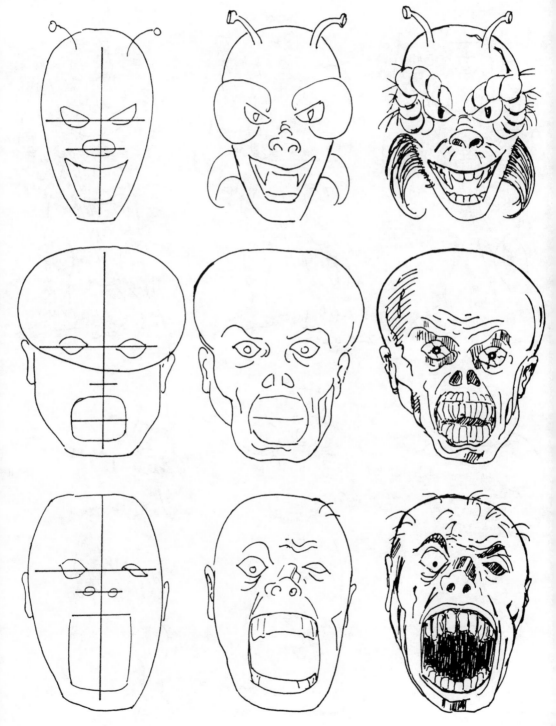

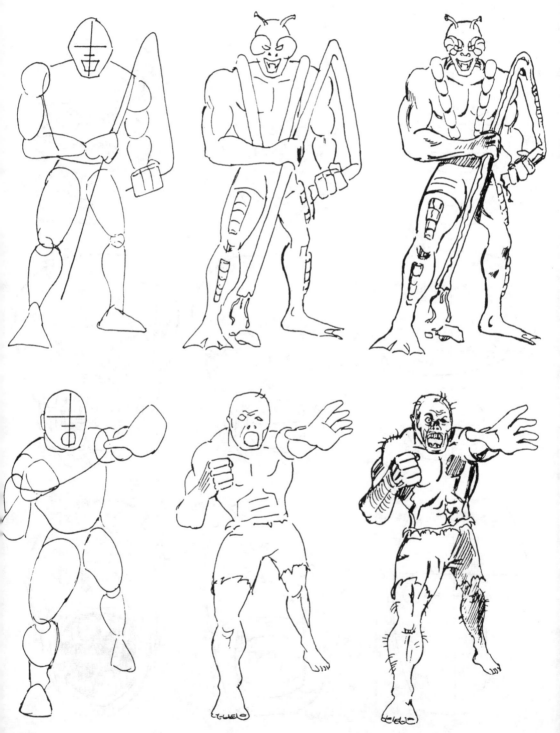

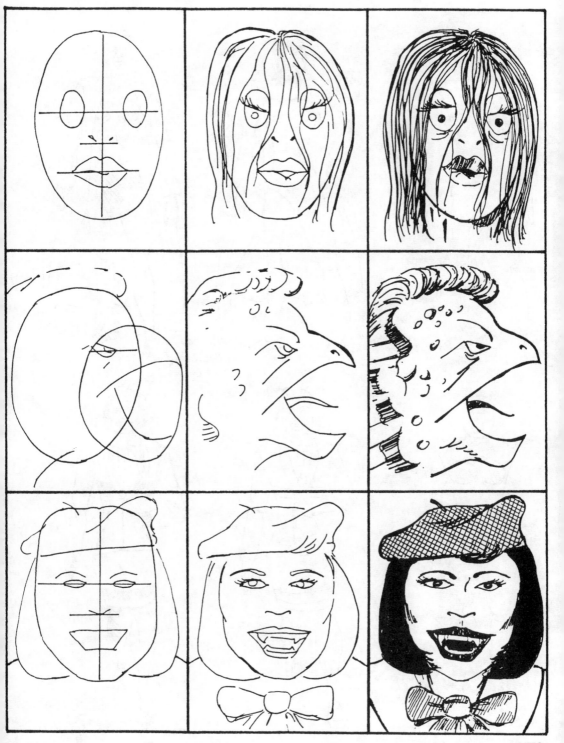

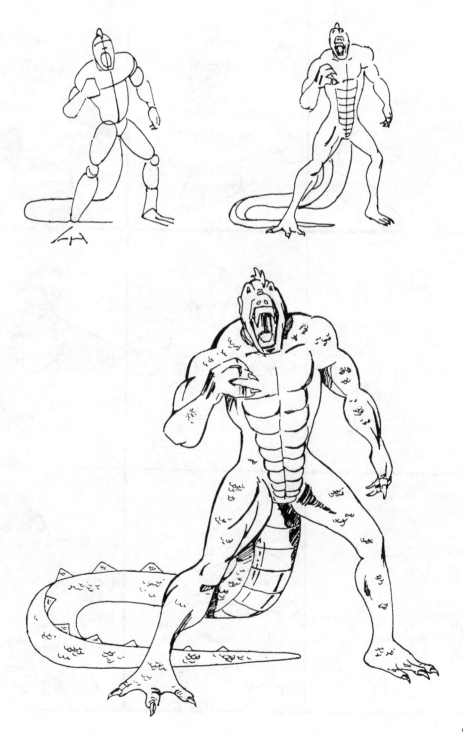

SUPERMONSTER BOXERS

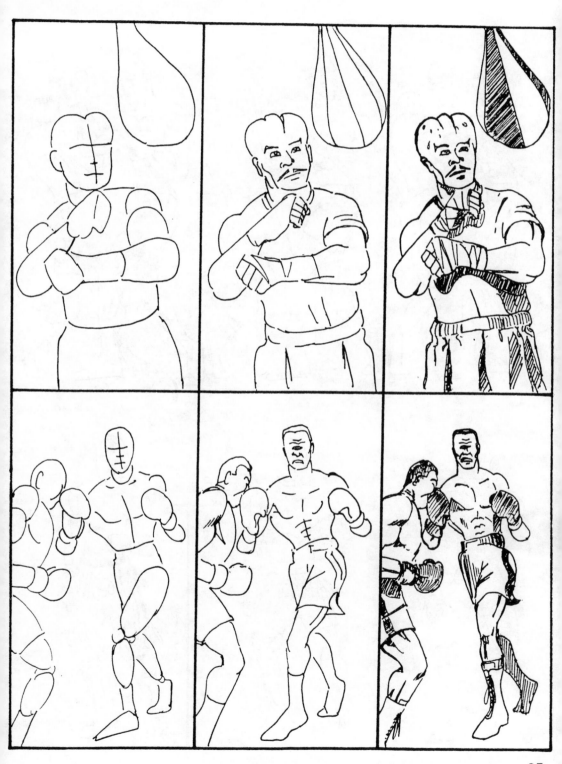

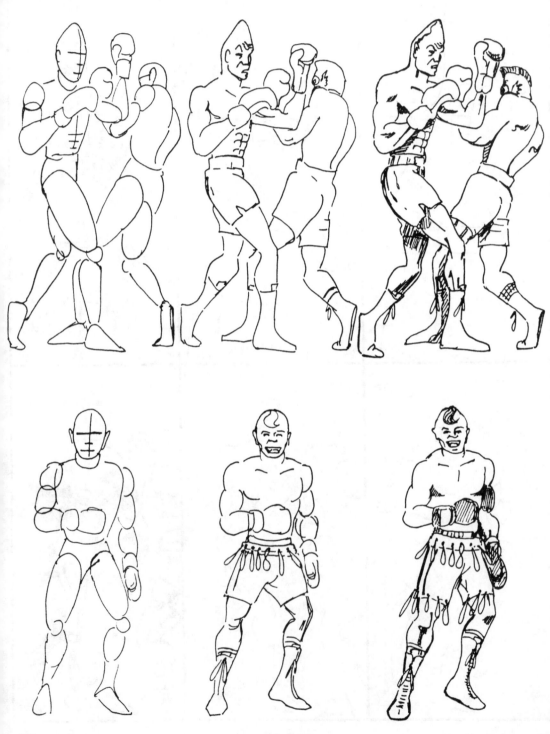

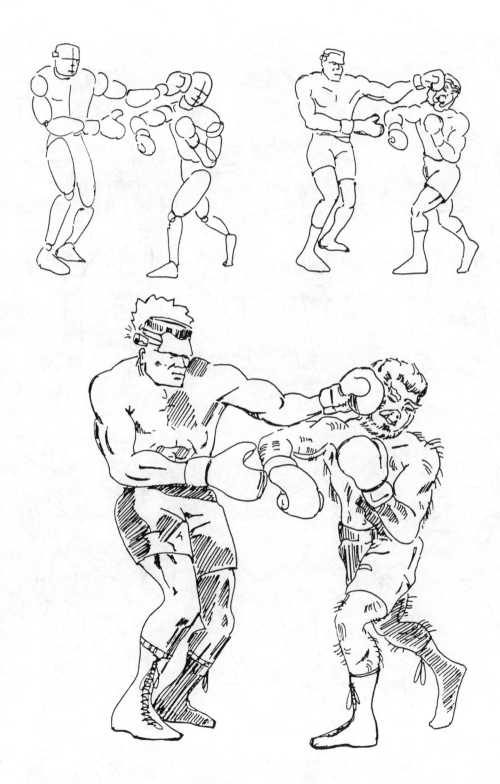

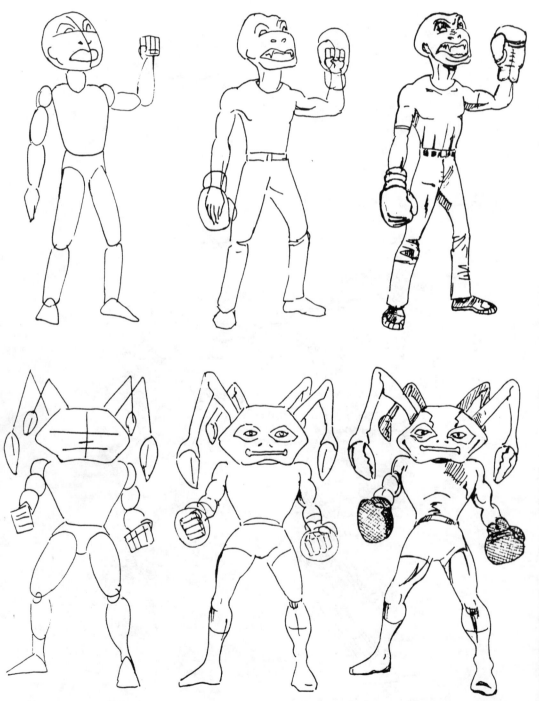